Accide

Necessities

Elle Selles

/ BookLeaf
Publishing

India | USA | UK

Presentation by *BookLeaf Publishing*

Web: www.bookleafpub.com

E-mail: info@bookleafpub.com

ISBN: 9789358314427

First edition 2023

For the author, who refuses to be known as
'poet'.

PREFACE

The sun is shining | The flowers are smiling.
Elle Selles, age four.

Forgot how to spell 'smelling'. The whimsy of
teachers took it from there.

It's always a morning

Like in that play: just mangled guts pretending.
Except that it's not
just my guts. I can feel my whole being loosen:
my legs slide away from my pelvis as my
hands slacken
knuckle by knuckle. My body: stretched taut
then snap
ped, loose and sloppy on the floor. My
s
p
i
n
e
has splintered and my skin torn, my joints come
apart and my intestines writhe, a rosy puddle
beside me. They're keeping me warm.
And
All the while the nerves keep firing, stuttering,
stalling, screaming. I can feel my legs, my
fingertips and my torso is intact where a whole
should be and there is no pain.
No blood.
" pressure.
" sensation.

My connective tissues have upped and gone and all I can think about is the slinky from Toy Story. Fuck knows where Buzz and Woody are now: in search of a new frontier; a better game to play rather; a more violent game to watch. Christ. This has all got a bit depressing. I tell my legs to move and they do.

Elegy

O, to be a ghost.
My bedsheet dragging on the floor.
My eyes in shadow and uneven.

I'd drift about the place.
Visiting who I wanted, watching what I dared.
I'd reach out my wispy fingers and fail to touch.

Wandering the hallways.
Wandering old words.
Wandering til I'm bored of space of gaps of
world.

The lack of real sensation.
Mind's hollow request fulfilled.
Only to wake again, bedsheet twisting my
ankles, eyes sealed with soot.

Oh to be a ghost, my friend, O to be a ghoul.

You're gone again.

You're gone again.
So I wave from the door,
Shut it behind you.
Close it like a cut.
Like a trench in the earth.

Because that's what's left.
This brave sadness.
Not the hopelessness
of depression
nor the anger of despair. But
sadness,
simple and infantilising.
Like trudging
through a downpour. Or
weeping
as
the
crescendo
builds.

It's the knowledge
that something is over
and
that you've nothing left to fight for.

It's the kind of pain
you get good
at feeling.
A loss we've always known.

And
All the while I'm a child
Again waiting at the
side of the playground, waiting for a friend.
And it's stupid
Because we were small then.
And now we're not.
But I can still feel you leaving.
There and
Gone.
Like you were before.

So I know it's not for
Ever.
We could never be so sure.
But I let slip the handle
Take a breath
Don't lock the door.

New Year's Eve

Because I feel like I'm falling apart
Like every time before
Because there is are times before
And if I was wrong then I probably am now.
And I don't want that.
I don't want this hope.
For once I want to feel like I'm falling
Apart and for it to be true
Or else leave
Me be.

New Year's Day

But I don't want the answers, just a hint
Or three, or four. to just catch my breath so
I can tell if it's a flea or just lint
Without such a sad revulsion to throw

Me overboard. To the wolves. Or off track.
Whatever that is, was, could be, because
I'm too young to whine. By my skin, my back
Is fine because because time healed what was.

I wish I'd had a choice in the matter
To let my flesh burn, to tear me apart.
Please, just, for once, bruise or splinter or break.
Leave me broken and not granted this part.

This isn't self loathing. I wish it were.
I'll write on love when hate's a lesser lure.

Hoar

The tree was raining.
Water tumbling down the birch's bare limbs,
catching on the paper bark
(sodden at the edges),
the drops ticking softly.
I heard the rain and watched the grass freeze it
white.

Sudden as a Sunrise

Sudden as a sunrise
I watch the hours
Fall into each other
As my fingers twitch and
Eyes drift down the hall
And I let the seconds pass by.

I feel my skin vibrating
Each cell calling my
Bluff my way through a meeting
And pacing down the hall
As I peel of my clothes, my
Hair and teeth, are sticky with it all.

Certain as a lightning strike
Normal as the
Fall to say it takes over me
Would be injustice, the gall
To think it is anything other?
How dare you, leave us be!
Sudden as the sunrise,
I let the others see.

I'm sorry, I had a dental appointment

And I know some people were talking the truth.
I know.
But I cannot could not cannot know
who, what, when, where, why.
But I know
people lie
when they're scared or panicked or bored and
that ruins people li(k)e me.

The Snakes

I used to dream of monsters.
Sleeping at a sprint
I'd hide and fight and wake when the jaws were
sinking in.

Then there were the people (hunters, killers all)
I knew how to fight them. I knew I would lose
and above the sun would blare.

After came the panic of
an empty suitcase a ticking clock and
eyes that could not open. A haze of grey and
green.

But before
There were snakes. Weaving the ground like
bugs or pests
Sinew and scale mazes unable to resolve.
And I'd watch
In terror
In acceptance alike.
I'd wait in sleep as the snakes slithered by.

Black

It leaks from the frame
Or behind you. Encroaching
Ever so gradually.
Or not so.
Because she is wearing that dress
When he opens the door.
Then it travels upwards, outwards
as the crow flies:
Beating and slow. Vulnerable
To noise- her cough among his
Laughter. Or so she thinks.
Then later, he walks with
It- fixed and frosting at the toe of his shoe,
increasing through her stocking
Skimming her thigh.
And then it holds the fly to the wall
When he opens the door.
Until he picks up the book.
(Switch on. Turn down.)
And he strips it from the pages.
Taking every letter and lie and
He makes it real
For her, in that dress.
With the look in his eyes.
And it is not

gradual as the smoke, fly, print
then stocking,
Are lost to the darkness as well

A Summary of Selected Friendships

In brief, and out of order.

1.
Beginning
Mid[80 miles]

2.
Begi-ddle
Middle
Mid
END!

3.
Beginning
End
Beginning
End
Beginning
Middle
Beginning

4.
Beginning?

Miiiiiddle
End

5.
Beginning
Middle
En-
Middle, definitely middle

6.
Middling
End

7.
B-end

8.
Beginning.......
Dead

9.
Beginning
Middle
[With regrets, The End]

10.
Beginning
Middle
(Please never) End

Barmaid

Some other woman in peril
Would see struggle here.
Between bottles and
Bar (flies) mats
The liquor festers
And falls from their
Mouths
Tongues
Teeth
And, eagerly,
I drink it all.

I do not sit,
That's not allowed
(They want to see my legs).
I pour two a drink while
The third, sips his dregs.
The man in the corner hates cider.
The woman beside him hates me.
I pluck up their coins
Their litter
Their lies
Wish them good day
They give up their pennys for free.

Darling, while you're down there…
Can I have a flake with that?
But did you hear that Joan's gone away?
The drains are revolting
They've painted it green
He's selling his car
The wife's making stew
Did you know Geoff couldn't pay?
I didn't but did you see-

Meet your new neighbour
Go talk to Vern, he knows all about Sarah,
The backdoor, the side door, the works.
Pay attention
My eyes are up here.
Now what did you say you want?
Saul has a bitch who needs breeding
Heidi knows who she knows
But they've always hated
Despised
Despaired
Oh how did Sy's story go?

I'll give them your card
His word
My time.
Who sells this crap?
The barrel's gone off
I think you'll find you're a fool

But I'd never sow that
I heard it from him!
Of course it's the truth and
Do you like gin?

I'll sow any seed you give me.
Water it? Well, as you're so nice.
I take care of my wares,
Yours' too, I guess
My way through the rest.
Doctoring, gardening,
- Floral! With notes of ginseng-
table flowers and fruit by the slice
Lay down the roots
Let the weeds come to light
Get a good grip
and pull until something
Do you like tonic?
Then pull until something snaps.

A Walk

Tedious as always: the zips, and laces, buckles
and ties.
Him waiting at the door, near whining, as she
catches my heels.
My headphone slipping from my waxen ear.
Glasses (sun not sight) slipping on my oily nose.
I'll shower next. Later.
For now we walk.
My sock is twisted and my coat ill-needed- I
take it off and throw it over the fence.
He stops, concerned for my loss, but with a tug
he trots on. I let her jolt ahead.
A lead in each hand, they weave amongst
themselves, the cords knitting together as my
tepid hands fail to keep up.
My shirt falls backwards from my shoulders,
tugging at my throat like a cape.
I pull the dogs back closer.
The sun isn't hitting yet and my ankle already
pulsing.
My hands rotate through their chores: exchange
leads; reinstate glasses; leads; T-shirt; refit
headphone; recall her.
I'm aching by the mile, before the pollen kicks
in.

On the grass the pulsing lessens. I loose the
dogs. I breathe.
I lower the volume and let the shit headphone
fall. Tuck it in my pocket for later.
She is in a hedge but I can hear her snorting. I
leave her be. He knows to stay close. Running,
rolling in the long grass, seed flecking his ears.
The path ahead opens out and the sun trickes in.
For once I haven't seen anyone.
For once, no one is near.
I lead them off course, past the nettles and
budding gorse.
He shouts ahead this time, exploring his new
frontier. She lingers in my shadow until a kite
races by.
I should be more careful- there are deer in the
wood. And around the bend, where the hill
descends, the badgers dig into the mud.
But he likes the roll in the buttercups. And she
chases the wind. And for once I'm not waiting
(to get it over with, to get it done).
So I breath my breathe and slow my stride.
It'll be over when I'm gone.

And I hope you know that I didn't want to lie and that I'm not really sure why I did if that helps)

Thank you for your message. I got it as I picked up
my bags to leave because I did have somewhere to
go- two places in fact- but I chose the one that
wasn't really the best choice but it made me
feel better at the time. And yes, I know I will have to
lie again later but honestly, I had a lovely morning.
I walked up the road, the one away from you, and headed
to the park I love but never actually visit because
I get to the top of the hill and then I remember
how life was this morning and that line
from that play becomes relevant again and I
can feel my knees working up the nerves to say
Fuck you! to me, not you. Thank you for your message
though, I'm sorry that I didn't feel guilty but
frankly,

we never arranged to meet and you didn't
message me last
week or the week before when I didn't even
have a decent
excuse so who was I to know really. But thanks,
for the
message, I hope I see you later and in fact I may
go to great
lengths to encourage it because as much as I
enjoyed my decision this morning, I feel lies (or
half-truths) work best when truly hammered
home.
So, I'll see you later, if you have time to fit me
in
where I normally wouldn't. I know you're busy
but you
sent me a message so I guess you'd like to see
me. And I'll tell you
about this morning and my decision and the
walk I took away
from you and towards that hill which I had no
intent of falling
down so I took a detour through the cemetery
where it
was still sunny and I'd never walked before.
That place
needs better treatment. It's beautiful, it really is,
but

Is was kind of difficult to tell what was path and
what was
grave. Odd dilemma to face of a morning but I
enjoyed the walk nonetheless. I'd recommend it
if it
weren't a strange thing to do and it wasn't
contradictory to
what I told you I was doing but I could weave
my words, I'm sure.
But it was nice, in the quiet, so I probably won't
tell you for
fear of bumping into someone I know whilst
walking through
a graveyard where I know none of the graves or
the people
in them. I pretended I did, of course; read a few
headstones,
meandered,
took several different paths to make it look like I
knew
where I was going but honestly, I was just trying
to get
out of the damn place because, pretty as it is, it
needs to be
looked after better because I couldn't really get
out once
I was in and I don't think it is appropriate for a
local charity

to trap people in graveyards even if they have no cause to be

there. I wouldn't have even gone in if it weren't for the hill and

all. And the trees were pretty, plus I saw a single crow and I'm

not superstitious but I felt it best to not push my luck, especially

after having lied to you. Well, not really lied, I did have something to do,

but then I decided to kill time in a graveyard which doesn't really

say a lot about me if I choose to do that instead of meeting you

and doing what I'm in the city for. And to be honest that's an

awful lot to fit in one message so I'm sorry, I'll see you later,

if you have time?

A Note on a Courtroom Drama

This has gotten drastically out of hand.
By that I mean I have no idea what is going on.
They're talking and I
think I should be listening but
it's all going over my head and
I don't (really) see what good that's going to
do seeing as he's already dead and all.
They're back in lawyery mode where
'taking the stand' means 'go
sit over there', and 'objection' means 'I'm
smarter
than you' and 'they were friends' means 'they
fucked'.
For all its worth we didn't.

The Fact of a Courtroom Drama

It's no trouble at all, really!
An email going back and fourth, it's tumbleweed of
Attachments catching on the edge of the frame but not enough to
Tear away from the focus the fold, the panic of it all.
A note becomes two becomes five becomes the step
In or/of a steer. A break, a pause, another job, another
Email on the horizon. Of a Tuesday in June.
"Administration Error"
Wednesday.
Cough
Thursday.
It's June. Heat.
The suit.
But the heat.
The suit. And a side room. Makeup too
Thick hair on the wrong side.
Tumbleweed.
Hurry up and wait-
Ing room.

No time to wait.

The stillness of the camera keeps him just out of
Frame of mind. Professional. Clean and clear.

Keep it simple,

Stupid question DON'T SAY THAT OUT
LOUD.

Breathe.

Yes, that it my understanding. Page 16? Yes, I'm
there. The defendant is asleep just out of
Frame of reference was declared as-

Facts facts facts facts could be possible probable
unlikely.

Page 17. That is the case.

Page 18. 19. Fifty four. Is this badgering yet? I
feel badgered.

Fifty five.

No?

Fifty six.

Okay still going.

Sixty two.

My god this is dull.

Conversation

Speak of the devil and he shall appear.
We are talking about you, how you feel. There
are no devils here.
And that's just the point, isn't it? Or haven't you
got it yet?
What do you mea-
Because I'm not the first and definitely not the
last.
What are you then?
It's nothing, that's the point.
You are not nothing.
I know. But that's not true.
You're not making any sense.
I know!
...
I don't make any sense.
And how does that make you feel.
Speak of the devil and he shall appear.
What do you mean by that?
Trigger.
Trigger? Like a gun?
Gun and target.
What does that mean?
What it says on the tin.
I don't think you're taking this seriously.

How do you know?

Because you aren't.

Again, how do you know?

…

Because I don't.

So, what's on your mind?

Everything and N-

And nothing?

Yes.

What do you mean by that?

What I think.

Yes. What do you think about that?

No.

No?

Exactly.

You need to start talking to me or-

Or what?

Or I can't help you.

How would you help me?

I will know when you tell me what is wrong.

Nothing.

Not this again. You're too old for this.

This is it.

And what do you mean by that?

You're not going to understand.

Try me.

I already have.

Moment One

The purpose of this pain is simple.
It's a reminder that I'm here.
That I'm breathing.
And that it will never go away.
(You're being a twat.
Eat something.
Have a nap.
Yes, you're still breathing.
Yes, you're still here.
But so are painkillers and therapy.
Get on with it).

Milton Keynes UK
Ingram Content Group UK Ltd.
UKHW020917300424
441987UK00015B/730

9 789358 314427